The Little Book of Props for Early Writing

Ideas for activities for the Foundation Stage

Written by Ann Roberts
Series editor Sally Featherstone

Illustrations by Alison Smith

The Little Book of Props for Early Writing
ISBN 1 904187 06 4

©Featherstone Education Ltd., 2002
Text ©Ann Roberts & Sally Featherstone, 2002

'Little Books' is a trade mark of Featherstone Education Ltd.

Published in the United Kingdom by
Featherstone Education Ltd.
44 - 46 High Street
Husbands Bosworth
Leicestershire
LE17 6LP

Environmental Information

This book is printed on paper manufactured in the European Community. It is made from the pulp of eucalyptus trees harvested from sustainable forests. It is more environmentally friendly than most recycled papers because it is produced without using chlorine. It is our policy to stipulate environmentally friendly stock for all our paper requirements. Featherstone Education Ltd.

Becoming a writer

Most children acquire speech naturally through interaction with adults and with the other children in their environment. In order to become a writer, a child has to develop the concept of messages. He/she then has to compose, present and scribe their message, using a range of physical and mental skills. The decoding and writing of symbols is a highly complicated activity, and children need an understanding of symbols in the environment and in written language before they can begin to imitate or replicate them. Of the four language modes (talking, listening, reading, and writing) writing is the most complex and the latest to develop.

Children in their early years learn best through play and imitation. They learn about the nature and purpose of writing by:

- observing adults and other children writing (models of writers)
- observing and noticing print in their environment (examples of writing)
- sending and receiving messages (cards, letters, postcards, notes) (recognising the purposes of writing as sending a message)
- observing writing in books and other written material (seeing the difference between pictures and print)
- experimenting with mark making and writing themselves ('having a go' and seeing themselves as writers).

Practitioners should ensure that they offer children all these opportunities, inside the setting, in the garden and in the local environment.

From a very young age, children begin to recognise the elements of writing, particularly those associated with their own names. They make marks which approximate the symbols they see - straight lines, radials, circles and dots all represent the letters they see. Wiggly lines, zigzags, rows of marks all represent the lines and blocks in our writing.

This stage is often referred to as 'emergent' writing, sometimes described as the 'apprentice' stage or 'have a go' stage. It develops best through first hand experience at home and in the setting. Opportunities for apprentice writing arise in all areas of learning and at all stages of development. Two vital components are supporting adults and interesting experiences which stimulate excitement, curiosity and imagination.

The purpose of this collection of ideas is to stimulate early writing through a range of situations, carefully introduced and modelled by practitioners and then offered to the children so they can develop the ideas in their free play and in writing in role.

Of course, in order to become confident and fluent writers, children also need to develop:

- confidence and an ability to take risks and make mistakes
- fine motor control and co-ordination
- hand-eye co-ordination
- skill in handling a range of tools
- recognition of pattern and shape
- the vocabulary of writing.

It is easy to be distracted from encouraging independence in writing. It is easy to confuse handwriting and creative writing. Handwriting is a skill, needing close supervision and clear instruction - it has to be <u>taught</u>. The writing described in this book is independent and is <u>learned</u> by confident children, who have been encouraged to experiment, explore, imitate and play with writing.

Here are some questions you might ask yourselves about writing in your setting:

? Is our setting full of lists, labels, notices, and charts - examples of writing in different forms?

? Are some of these written by children?

? Does our role play area have relevant writing materials - pens, pads, forms, jotters, appointment books?

? Do we use magazines, junk mail, cookery books, lists, posters to demonstrate a range of writing? Is this in a range of languages?

? Have we made writing and reading spaces in our setting? Do children and adults use them?

? Are we models of adults as writers? Do we write where children can see us?

? Do we provide writing and mark making implements - pens, pencils, clip boards, white boards, paper, envelopes, computers?

? Does writing happen indoors and out?

and most of all - **is writing fun?**

Links with the Early Learning Goals

Here are some of the goals which will be covered during the writing activities described in this book.

IN PERSONAL, SOCIAL & EMOTIONAL DEVELOPMENT
- be confident to try new activities, initiate ideas & speak in a familiar group;
- work as part of a group or class, taking turns & sharing fairly, understanding that there need to be agreed values, & codes of behaviour for groups of people, including adults & children, to work together harmoniously;
- select & use activities & resources independently.

IN LANGUAGE, COMMUNICATION AND LITERACY
- interact with others, negotiating plans & activities, taking turns in conversations;
- enjoy listening to and using spoken and written language, and readily turn to it in their play and learning;
- listen with enjoyment and respond to stories, songs, and other music, rhymes and poems and make up their own stories, rhymes and poems;
- extend their vocabulary, exploring the meanings & sounds of new words;
- speak clearly & audibly with confidence & control & show awareness of the listener, for example by their use of conventions such as 'please' & 'thank you';
- use language to imagine & recreate roles & experiences;
- use talk to organise, sequence & clarify thinking, ideas, feelings & events;
- use their phonic knowledge to write simple regular words & make phonetically plausible attempts at more complex words;
- explore and experiment with sounds, words and texts;
- read a range of familiar & common words & simple sentences independently;
- know that print carries meaning, & in English, is read from left to right & top to bottom
- show an understanding of elements of stories, such as main character, sequence of events, openings, & how information can be found in non fiction texts, to answer questions about where, who, why & how;
- attempt writing for various purposes, using features of different forms such as lists, stories, instructions;
- write their own names and labels & form sentences, sometimes using punctuation
- use a pencil effectively & hold it effectively to form recognisable letters, most of which are correctly formed.

IN KNOWLEDGE & UNDERSTANDING OF THE WORLD
- find out about past & present events in their own lives and in those of their families & other people they know;
- observe, find out & identify features in the place they live & the natural world.

IN CREATIVE DEVELOPMENT
- use their imagination in art & design, music, dance, imaginative & role play & stories.

Contents

Focus of the page   **page number**

Introduction	3,4,5
How may I help you?	8 and 9
Bag it!	10 and 11
Lets go on a visit!	12 and 13
Make a plate	14 and 15
I've got to make a ticket or two	16 and 17
Lost and found	18 and 19
Don't forget!	20 and 21
Wish you were here!	22 and 23
The Magic Cookbook	24 and 25
Can I take a message?	26 and 27
Signs of writing	28 and 29
I like it!	30 and 31
Seeds 'R' Us	32 and 33
All about me	34 and 35
Ouch!	36 and 37
Fire, police, ambulance!	38 and 39
Can we build it?	40 and 41
Long, long ago	42 and 43
Send a message	44 and 45
Want2talk?	46 and 47
Going my way?	48 and 49
So many languages	50 and 51
Secrets and spies	52 and 53
RSVP	54 and 55
In character	56 and 57
Make a list	58 and 59
Journey of a toy	60 and 61
Our new ducklings	62 and 63
When can you come?	64 and 65

How may I help you?

Turn your home area into a hotel or bed and breakfast. Then set up a booking in desk to encourage writing.

Resources

* calendar or diary
* checking in book
* calculator, computer
* cash register or cash drawer
* keys with tags or old swipe cards
* message pad and pens
* phone, pager
* paper and envelopes
* name badges
* pigeonholes or board with numbered hooks for keys

Furniture & layout

* reception desk, table or shelf
* swivel chair
* chairs for waiting
* luggage
* trolleys
* notice board
* open/closed sign
* hotel brochures
* travel leaflets

NB. you can collect leaflets of local attractions from most hotel foyers, even if you are not staying there!

Starting points and stimuli

1. Give the children time to talk about what it's like to stay in a hotel. Join in with your experiences.
2. Talk through the sequence of checking in.
3. Try to visit a hotel, find out first when it's a good time to visit!
4. Model some of the activities, verbally and the writing bits, such as welcoming a guest, filling in forms, signing in, finding keys, writing bills etc.
5. Practise taking calls and messages, booking taxis, telephone conventions.
6. Collect and display the specialist words for this activity.
7. Use writing for labels, lists, memos, menus, messages.

Extension activities:

1. Make a restaurant and take orders for meals.
2. Make a room service menu (with pictures and words) and order from your hotel room.
3. Booking a taxi to take you to the station or airport.

Vocabulary

- How can I help you?
- How long are you staying?
- Sign here please
- key
- keycard
- Reception
- lift
- luggage
- bedroom
- bathroom
- shower
- balcony
- television
- pool
- restaurant
- room service
- bill
- credit card
- message

Early Learning Goals

* interact with others, negotiating plans & activities & taking turns in conversations;
* speak clearly & audibly with confidence & control;
* attempt writing for various purposes;
* use a pencil effectively & hold it effectively to form recognisable letters;
* recognise numerals 1-9.

Bag it!

Text on shopping bags is an easily accessible source of inspiration for children's own early writing. Turn part of your creative area into a bag factory, and personalise some bags.

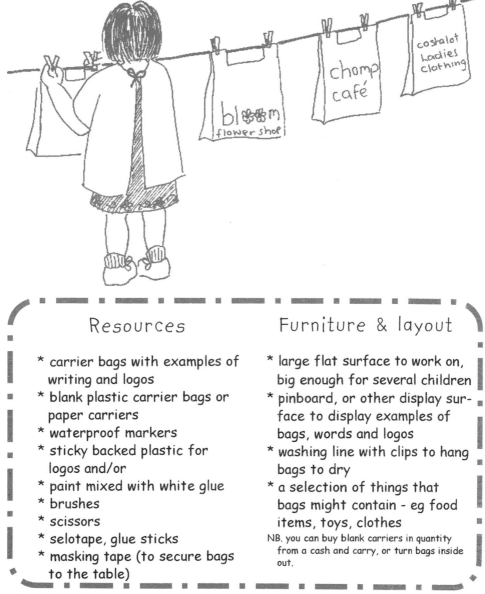

Resources

* carrier bags with examples of writing and logos
* blank plastic carrier bags or paper carriers
* waterproof markers
* sticky backed plastic for logos and/or
* paint mixed with white glue
* brushes
* scissors
* selotape, glue sticks
* masking tape (to secure bags to the table)

Furniture & layout

* large flat surface to work on, big enough for several children
* pinboard, or other display surface to display examples of bags, words and logos
* washing line with clips to hang bags to dry
* a selection of things that bags might contain - eg food items, toys, clothes

NB. you can buy blank carriers in quantity from a cash and carry, or turn bags inside out.

Starting points and stimuli

1. Collect some items in a bag and talk about how you might label the bag and where you might have bought them.
2. Collect some carriers and bags from local shops and major chains. Talk with the children about the way pictures and writing are used to convey messages. Guess what comes in each bag.
3. Talk about slogans, symbols, trademarks. Start with easily recognised ones such as MacDonalds, Toys R Us, Tesco, Disney Store, Early Learning.
4. Model how you might invent a slogan or a logo for your own name or a shop you owned.

Extension activities:

1. Set up a role play shop and make your own bags, signs and notices.
2. Look at adverts and signs in newspapers and junk mail.
3. Go for a shop walk and spot signs and logos in your area.
4. Use computer clip art to make logos and signs.

Vocabulary

- trade marks
- sale
- value
- shop
- toys
- baby
- clothes
- supermarket
- best
- buy
- bikes
- shop
- save
- good
- food
- phone
- www.
- street
- flowers
- fruit

Early Learning Goals

* attempt writing for various purposes;
* know that print carries meaning;
* select tools & techniques they need;
* observe, find out & identify features in the place they live;
* express and communicate their ideas through designing and making.

11

Let's go on a visit!

Before you go on a walk, visit or other excursion, use the planning and anticipation as a stimulus for writing.

Resources

* calendars and diaries
* strips of paper for lists
* maps and plans of the area
* leaflets and descriptions of the place you are visiting
* pens, pencils, crayons
* backpack or other bag with the things you need
* lunchbox, beach bag etc
* photos, pictures, books or miniatures of the things you may see.

Furniture & layout

* table, preferably with a pinboard or wall behind; chairs
* display of pictures
* room to spread out maps, plans and larger pieces of paper
* notice board with words
* one or two relevant items, such as a beachball, zoo animal, map, picnic box

NB. tourist information centres are good sources of information about your own community or other places

Starting points and stimuli

1. Introduce the discussion of the visit in plenty of time for anticipation and planning. Discuss when, where and why you are going.
2. Talk through the sequence of planning for a trip.
3. Look at maps, plans and pictures together.
4. Talk about lists and reminders, and model how to write and use them.
5. Take suggestions from the children of what you need to take, to collect, to research before you go.
6. Use travel guides and information leaflets to help children with prediction and planning - 'What if..' 'What do we need for....'.

Extension activities:

1. Use small world sets to stimulate talk about the visit and to 'walk through' what might happen.
2. Use the opportunity to make tickets, build with bricks, make big maps outside with playground chalk.

Vocabulary

◆ Name of the place you are visiting. Perhaps on a signpost.
◆ Relevant vocabulary, eg zoo animals, seaside words.

◆ visit	◆ wellies
◆ bus	◆ map
◆ sandwiches	◆ dinner
◆ ticket	◆ picnic
◆ backpack	◆ camera
◆ first aid	◆ ice cream
◆ jacket	◆ souvenir

Early Learning Goals

* interact with others, negotiating plans & activities;
* extend their vocabulary;
* use talk to organise, sequence & clarify thinking, ideas, feelings & events;
* attempt writing for various purposes, such as lists, instructions;
* use a pencil effectively & hold it effectively to form recognisable letters.

Make a plate

Here is a good reason for writing! Make some number plates for the outside toys or miniature plates for small world play

Resources

* sample number plates
* car magazines and leaflets
* number and letter stencils
* jotters and pads
* white or yellow card cut in rectangles
* photos of number plates
* thick pens
* hole punch, string, scissors
* brochures and leaflets
* stickers for little number plates

Furniture & layout

* large workshop table (you could have this activity out-side or near the door)
* display board for examples of number plates,
* a sign with" Number Plate workshop"
* open/closed sign
* washing line or trellis and pegs to hang plates for drying

NB. you could try your local car showroom or Yellow Pages for leaflets and old number plates

Starting points and stimuli

1. Go for a walk or stand at the gate or fence and look at number plates. Look for number plates in books, photos, catalogues, brochures. Talk about capital letters.
2. Collect numbers from children's own cars in a Number Plate Book. Add staff car numbers.
3. Talk about the collections of letters and numbers and how they are arranged. Look for unusual number plates that say (or almost say) words. Discuss GB and other national plates and badges. Talk about number plates from different countries.
4. Try to get some real plates and look at how they are made. Talk about the different colours of number plates on the front and back of vehicles.
5. Attach the plates to wheeled toys and other vehicles.

Extension activities:

1. Play a number plate game where children try to say a word starting with each letter on the plate.

Vocabulary

◆ The major vocabulary in this activity will be capital letters and numbers from 0 to 9.

- ◆ open
- ◆ closed
- ◆ heavy goods
- ◆ lorry
- ◆ car
- ◆ ambulance
- ◆ van
- ◆ caravan
- ◆ trailer
- ◆ bike
- ◆ truck
- ◆ number

Early Learning Goals

* link letters & sounds, naming & sounding all letters of the alphabet;
* attempt writing for various purposes;
* use a pencil effectively & hold it effectively to form recognisable letters;
* recognise numerals 1-9;
* say and use number names in order in familiar contexts.

I've got to make a ticket or two.

Children love making tickets. Give them a format and a place to work and they will be off!

Resources

* card pieces, different sizes and colours
* stamps with pictures and designs
* hole punch, stapler
* pens and other markers
* paper clips
* scissors (plain and with patterned edges)
* calendar to help with dates
* plastic wallets/containers
* rolls of paper

Furniture & layout

* table or desk
* waste paper basket for the rejects
* display board with posters and other information about tickets
* words and phrases
* example forms and tickets
* open/closed sign

NB. Use paper till rolls from a stationer's or make your own and perforate the tickets with a sewing machine with no cotton in.

Starting points and stimuli

1. Collect some tickets yourself and ask the parents and children to contribute to the collection. Make a scrapbook for reference. Collect tickets from buses and trains, concerts, cinema, museums, zoos, holidays, pantomimes, shows, supermarket delicatessen, raffles etc.
2. Talk about why you need tickets. What is on a ticket. Look at your collection and note similarities and differences. Look at dates, times, prices, half price, children's tickets, pictures and designs.
3. Introduce the children to the ticket making area and talk about what it offers. Let the children experiment first before introducing any more formal activities.

Extension activities:

1. Make a ticket office front from an empty carton, and set up a box office.
2. Have a concert, show or exhibition and make the tickets for it. You could have booking forms and phone booking.

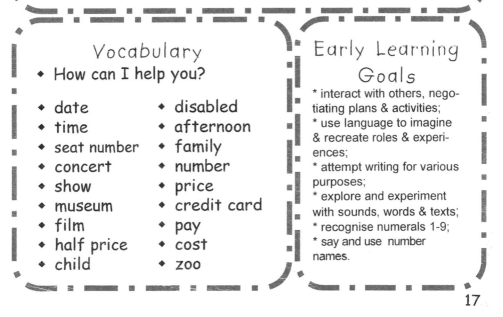

Vocabulary

* How can I help you?

* date
* time
* seat number
* concert
* show
* museum
* film
* half price
* child

* disabled
* afternoon
* family
* number
* price
* credit card
* pay
* cost
* zoo

Early Learning Goals

* interact with others, negotiating plans & activities;
* use language to imagine & recreate roles & experiences;
* attempt writing for various purposes;
* explore and experiment with sounds, words & texts;
* recognise numerals 1-9;
* say and use number names.

Lost and Found

Read Dogger or This is The Bear as a starter for a lost and found focus, making labels and lists. you could even use the lost property box from your setting!

Resources

* luggage tags
* labels, postcards
* card cut for own labels
* hole punch, string, safety pins
* message pad and pens
* phone
* paper for lists and posters
* clip boards
* boxes to sort the lost things
* Lost and Found book
* pictures and words
* story books

Furniture & layout

* reception desk, table or shelf
* chair
* pin board
* boxes, trolley or other storage
* baskets
* notice board
* open/closed sign

NB. Look in local papers and post offices or shops for lost and found notices.

Starting points and stimuli

1. Read the children a story or two about being lost or losing something. Talk about the feelings and what you do to find something lost.
2. Go to the local shops and see if you can find some lost and found notices. Look in local and free papers.
3. Set up a lost and found centre in a corner of the room with boxes for different sorts of things, and for new things/labelled things.
4. Model some of the activities, verbally and in writing, such as filling in the log book, writing labels and attaching them, taking phone calls, responding to callers.
5. Work alongside the children sometimes, helping them to sequence and sort out the activity.
6. Make overnight additions to the Found Basket, or leave something of your own outside or in the room to be found.

<u>Extension activities:</u>

1. Make some posters for the Parents board or the door.

Vocabulary

* How can I help you? What have you lost?

* lost
* found
* garden
* label
* classroom
* road
* toy
* jumper

* shoes
* plimsols
* shorts
* teeshirt
* book
* glasses
* purse
* keys

Early Learning Goals

* use language to imagine & recreate roles & experiences;
* write names and labels;
* use a pencil effectively & hold it effectively to form recognisable letters;
* extend their vocabulary, exploring the meanings & sounds of new words.

Don't forget!

Learning to make lists and write reminders is another way of encouraging children to see the purpose of writing.

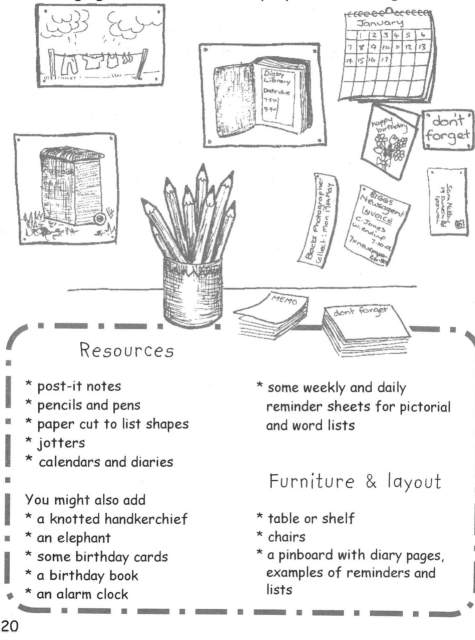

Resources

* post-it notes
* pencils and pens
* paper cut to list shapes
* jotters
* calendars and diaries

You might also add
* a knotted handkerchief
* an elephant
* some birthday cards
* a birthday book
* an alarm clock

* some weekly and daily reminder sheets for pictorial and word lists

Furniture & layout

* table or shelf
* chairs
* a pinboard with diary pages, examples of reminders and lists

Starting points and stimuli

1. You could read story such as 'Don't Forget the Bacon'.
2. Talk about the sorts of things people forget and need reminding about. Include shopping lists, reminders for special occasions such as birthdays, regular chores such as putting out the rubbish or recycling, returning library books and videos, collecting dry cleaning, dental appointments.
3. Ask the children what things they need to remember and how they remind themselves. Bringing their book back to school, which day is PE, bringing their lunch box, taking their coat home etc.
4. Tell them how you remember things, and model this with stickers or notes to remind yourself. Encourage them to help you by asking them to remind you of a letter needing posting, something you will bring to show them. Talk about picture, word and object prompts such as elephants.
5. Go through a day or week in the setting and make a reminder list, calendar or set of picture clues.

Vocabulary

* reminder
* list
* label
* sticker
* remember
* bring
* take
* do
* fetch
* birthday
* dentist
* doctor
* party
* visit
* forget

Early Learning Goals

* listen with enjoyment and respond to stories;
* use talk to organise, sequence & clarify thinking;
* know that print carries meaning;
* attempt writing for various purposes;
* use a pencil effectively & hold it effectively to form recognisable letters.

Wish you were here!

Sending a postcard is good fun, even if you are sending it to yourself or one of your friends!

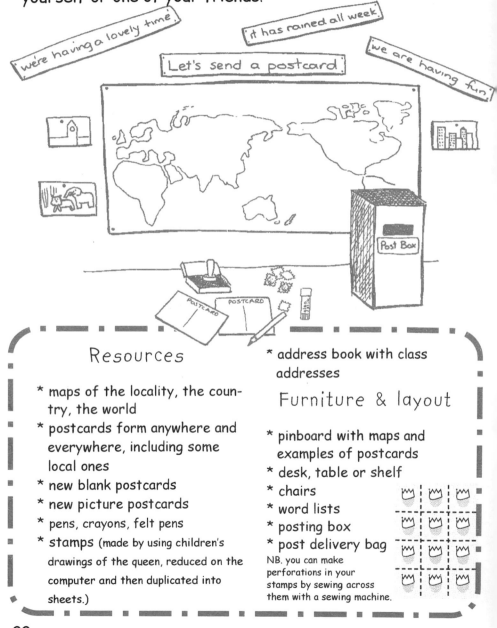

we're having a lovely time

it has rained all week

Let's send a postcard

we are having fun

Post Box

Resources

* maps of the locality, the country, the world
* postcards form anywhere and everywhere, including some local ones
* new blank postcards
* new picture postcards
* pens, crayons, felt pens
* stamps (made by using children's drawings of the queen, reduced on the computer and then duplicated into sheets.)
* address book with class addresses

Furniture & layout

* pinboard with maps and examples of postcards
* desk, table or shelf
* chairs
* word lists
* posting box
* post delivery bag

NB. you can make perforations in your stamps by sewing across them with a sewing machine.

Starting points and stimuli

1. Ask parents, children and friends to help you make a collection of postcards. Include local scenes, art cards, animals and people. Talk about why and when you send postcards and who you send them to.
2. Talk about and model the sort of things you might say on a card, including the weather and other events.
3. Suggest that children might like to make their own cards by drawing the pictures as well as writing.
4. Show them how to use the class address book to decide who the card should go to. Arrange a postbox and delivery service for the cards.
5. Encourage children to send postcards to the class when they go on holiday or on visits.
6. Make a pigeon hole for each child from shoe boxes.

Extension activities:

1. Use a digital camera to make your own postcards with children's pictures or photos of your setting.

Vocabulary

- good time
- dear
- post
- rain
- sun
- beach
- swimming
- camping
- caravan
- hotel
- family
- aeroplane
- car
- ice cream
- funfair
- museum
- exhibition
- trip
- holiday
- miss you

Early Learning Goals

* use language to imagine & recreate roles & experiences;
* use their phonic knowledge;
* attempt writing for various purposes;
* use a pencil effectively & hold it effectively to form recognisable letters;
* observe, find out about the place where they live.

The Magic Cookbook

Cook up some strange recipes and make a group cookbook or recipe file.

whisk spoon sieve

mix

Wormburger

terrible trifle

beat

stir

Ingredients:
1 big bun
lots of worms

Ingredients
mayonnaise
ketchup
potatoes

mash

our strange recipes

Resources

* cookery books of all sorts
* card or paper for recipes
* glue stick, pens, crayons etc
* some paper with borders (printed on the computer)
* photos and clip art of ingredients
* big book or file box for finished recipes
* pictures/photos and real implements - whisks, spoons, scales, pans etc

Furniture & layout

* desk, table or shelf
* chairs
* display board
* pictures of food or strange food made up on the computer
* bowls and spoons so they can imagine making their recipes
* aprons and chef's hats

NB. clip photo are good for this project

Starting points and stimuli

1. Use children's experience of cooking in your setting or at home to talk about food and recipes.
2. Read some cooking stories (eg Little Red Hen, Meg and Mog, Oliver's Vegetables)
3. Look at recipe books and show the children how they are constructed - with ingredients and methods.
4. Model making a recipe, mixing, counting, weighing - either a real or an imaginary recipe.
5. Talk about strange food names like Toad in the Hole, Pigs in blankets and Shepherd's Pie and what might be in them.
6. Offer a selection of unusual ingredients for cooking.

<u>Extension activities:</u>

1. Try making a new version of an old favourite - new yogurt flavours, new cakes or soups.
2. Make pictorial recipes by drawing the finished food and labelling the ingredients in the picture.
3. Make a new menu for a restaurant for giants or fairies.

Vocabulary

- cook
- apron
- measure
- recipe
- ingredients
- mix
- stir
- pour
- bake
- add
- count
- decorate
- cover
- fry
- cut
- boil
- whisk
- share
- spoon
- scales

Early Learning Goals

* enjoy listening to and using spoken and written language, and readily turn to it in their play and learning;
* explore and experiment with texts;
* attempt writing for various purposes;
* use talk to organise, sequence & clarify thinking, ideas, feelings & events.

Can I take a message?

Using the telephone is at the centre of this activity.
Providing message pads and pens will extend the enjoyment.

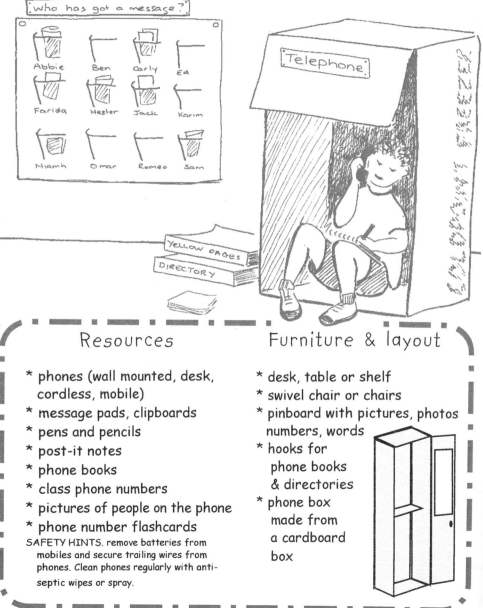

Resources

* phones (wall mounted, desk, cordless, mobile)
* message pads, clipboards
* pens and pencils
* post-it notes
* phone books
* class phone numbers
* pictures of people on the phone
* phone number flashcards

SAFETY HINTS. remove batteries from mobiles and secure trailing wires from phones. Clean phones regularly with antiseptic wipes or spray.

Furniture & layout

* desk, table or shelf
* swivel chair or chairs
* pinboard with pictures, photos numbers, words
* hooks for phone books & directories
* phone box made from a cardboard box

Starting points and stimuli

1. Look at different sorts of phones.
2. Visit the school office or other offices to watch how people answer the phone and take messages.
3. Model answering the phone yourself. Take messages and notes.
4. Encourage the children to use the phone freely before you introduce more formal activities.
5. Put up photos of children, staff and other adults and hang clips underneath each for messages.
6. Model looking up numbers in a phone book or directory.
7. Talk about how to leave a message as well as take a message.

Extension activities:

1. Discuss alphabetical order and display an alphabet line to help.
2. Borrow an answering machine for a day.
3. Make some message sheets on the computer and let the children suggest what they need to look like and contain.

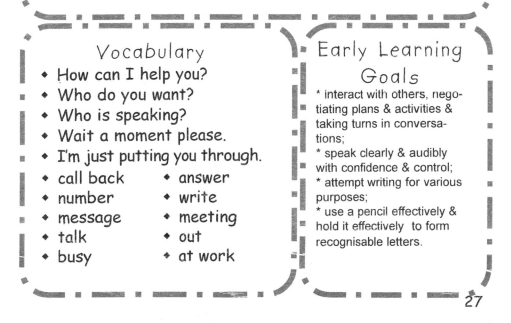

Vocabulary

- How can I help you?
- Who do you want?
- Who is speaking?
- Wait a moment please.
- I'm just putting you through.
- call back   • answer
- number   • write
- message   • meeting
- talk   • out
- busy   • at work

Early Learning Goals

* interact with others, negotiating plans & activities & taking turns in conversations;
* speak clearly & audibly with confidence & control;
* attempt writing for various purposes;
* use a pencil effectively & hold it effectively to form recognisable letters.

Signs of writing

Take a walk and look for signs and notices before you set up this writing area. Remember to take a camera with you.

Resources

* photos and other pictures of signs, road signs, street signs, directions, shop signs, notices, warnings etc
* examples of different sorts of fonts and writing
* card cut in squares, rectangles, circles, triangles
* pencils, crayons, paint, thick felt pens, scissors, glue
* stamps, stickers, borders
* number, letter stencils & stamps

Furniture & layout

* desk, table or shelf
* computer and printer if possible
* a file with photos and examples of different signs and notices
* key words to help in capitals and lower case
* pinboard or wall with signs displayed

NB. road maps, atlases and the Highway Code all have signs to stimulate discussion and for models

Starting points and stimuli

1. Take walks in your locality to look for signs and notices. Try to find some road works, traffic lights, road signs.
2. Talk about signs and notices they know, their purposes and meanings.
3. Talk about the colours and shapes of different signs, triangles, circles, red, blue, yellow.
4. Use small world sets to practise what happens when drivers and pedestrians see signs. Model how to make signs for small world sets (road works, police, accidents, airport)
5. Use the computer to make signs and print them out.

Extension activities:

1. Make some signs together for the garden, the classroom, the whole building.
2. Make some picture or symbol signs.
3. Make dual language signs.
4. Look in books, papers, catalogues, magazines for pictures of signs. Make a scrap book.

Vocabulary

- to the beach
- Road works
- Avenue
- Reception
- This way
- Exit
- Car Park
- Toilets
- Police
- Street
- Road
- Avenue
- School
- Children
- No Entry
- square
- triangle
- circle
- Parking

Early Learning Goals

* find out about their environment;
* attempt writing for various purposes;
* use a pencil effectively & hold it effectively to form recognisable letters;
* recognise numerals 1-9;
* - observe, find out & identify features in the place they live;
* use language such as circle to describe shapes.

I Like It!

Discuss likes and dislikes, then have a go at making lists of pictures or pictures and writing.

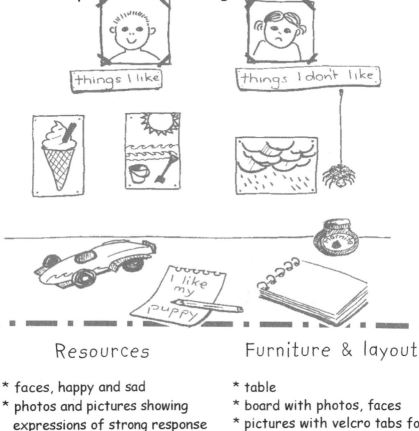

Resources

* faces, happy and sad
* photos and pictures showing expressions of strong response
* word bank of themed words (food, toys, places, things, games)
* feely box
* favourite toys (teddies, TV toys, clothing etc)
* catalogues and magazines
* paper and home made books
* pens, crayons, scissors

Furniture & layout

* table
* board with photos, faces
* pictures with velcro tabs for sticking and sorting into circles
* paper plates to sort onto
* food packets, toy packaging
* baskets or boxes to sort into

Starting points and stimuli

1. Do plenty of talking about things they like and dislike. Discuss feelings, food, toys, times of day, places etc.
2. Talk about and draw or write your likes and dislikes.
3. Discuss how one person's favourite is not the same as someone else's.
4. Read some stories about likes and dislikes - Mr Rabbit and the Lovely Present, Peace at Last.
5. Draw pictures of favourite outfits, meals etc
6. Collect and display the specialist words for this activity.

Extension activities:

1. Make a flannel graph or Velcro board with food items, dressing figures, toys to sort into circles.
2. Make some simple block graphs or diagrams to record favourite colours, breakfast cereals, pizza toppings. Model simple ways of writing what the graphs tell you.
3. Use a painting easel or clipboards to collect information about favourite activities inside or in the garden.

Vocabulary

- like
- love
- favourite
- best
- don't
- scare
- food
- toy
- clothes
- programme
- place
- colour
- holiday
- flavour
- smell
- taste
- sound
- picture

Early Learning Goals

* attempt writing for various purposes, using features of different forms such as lists;
* know that print carries meaning;
* use a pencil effectively & hold it effectively to form recognisable letters;
* talk about features they like and dislike.

31

Seeds R Us.

Use beans, peas and other dried seeds and nuts to make a seed shop or garden centre.

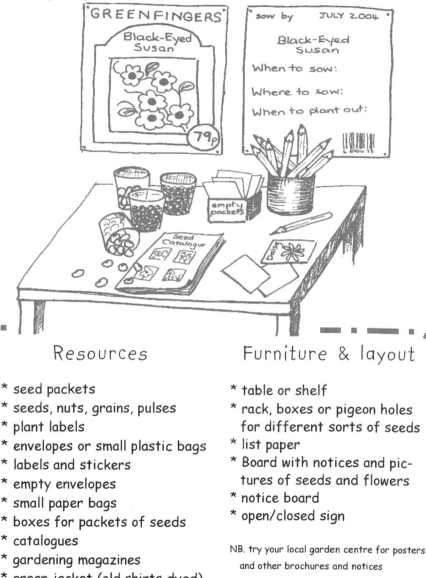

Resources

* seed packets
* seeds, nuts, grains, pulses
* plant labels
* envelopes or small plastic bags
* labels and stickers
* empty envelopes
* small paper bags
* boxes for packets of seeds
* catalogues
* gardening magazines
* green jacket (old shirts dyed)
  with badges

Furniture & layout

* table or shelf
* rack, boxes or pigeon holes
  for different sorts of seeds
* list paper
* Board with notices and pictures of seeds and flowers
* notice board
* open/closed sign

NB. try your local garden centre for posters
and other brochures and notices

Starting points and stimuli

1. If possible, visit a garden centre with the children, or take some photos to discuss.
2. Collect some gardening brochures, seed catalogues and magazines. You could write some letters with the children, or phone a few numbers for seed and bulb catalogues.
3. Make a sign for your seed shop and help the children to decorate the backing board.
4. Look carefully at the seed packets and the different types of seeds and flowers depicted on them.
5. Work alongside the children when they start, so you can model the activity of decorating and filling the packets.
6. Make a list of the different sorts of seeds on sale.

Extension activities:

1. Turn the seed factory into a shop. Write prices on the packets and sell them.
2. Try growing some of the seeds. Make a diary in a zig zag book of what happens as they grow.

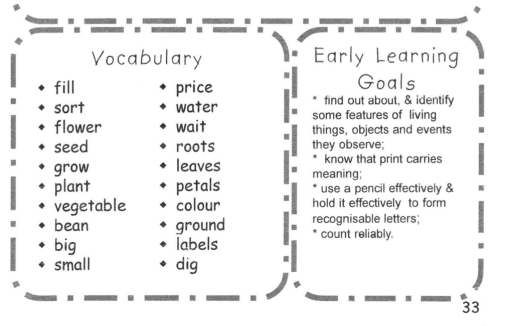

Vocabulary

- fill
- sort
- flower
- seed
- grow
- plant
- vegetable
- bean
- big
- small
- price
- water
- wait
- roots
- leaves
- petals
- colour
- ground
- labels
- dig

Early Learning Goals

* find out about, & identify some features of living things, objects and events they observe;
* know that print carries meaning;
* use a pencil effectively & hold it effectively to form recognisable letters;
* count reliably.

All about me

Provide the props for children to write about themselves, collecting personal details, writing diaries, making appointments, sorting out and organising their lives.

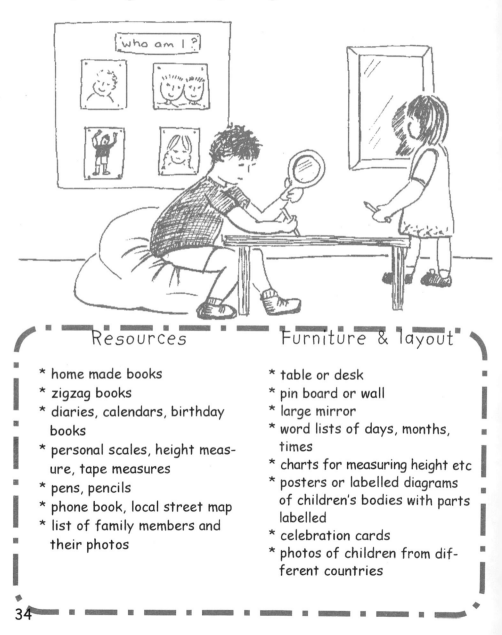

Resources

* home made books
* zigzag books
* diaries, calendars, birthday books
* personal scales, height measure, tape measures
* pens, pencils
* phone book, local street map
* list of family members and their photos

Furniture & layout

* table or desk
* pin board or wall
* large mirror
* word lists of days, months, times
* charts for measuring height etc
* posters or labelled diagrams of children's bodies with parts labelled
* celebration cards
* photos of children from different countries

Starting points and stimuli

1. Talk about and compare different features, hair and skin colour, birthday months, shoe sizes, heights etc.
2. Compare vital statistics and make charts.
3. Try making some finger prints with a stamp pad. Talk about the fact that everyone's finger print unique.
4. Use mirrors to help the children to look at and record their own features.
5. Collect individual information in class collections - phone numbers, addresses, birthdays etc.
6. Encourage children to make their own books about themselves with their chosen information.

Extension activities:

1. Link the activity to some outside challenges in running, jumping, throwing etc. Collect results on clipboards or a flip chart.
2. Take some digital photos of the children and use them to inspire writing..

Vocabulary

- hair
- eyes
- height
- tall
- black
- brown
- blue
- green
- short
- long

- months of the year
- days of the week
- birthday
- date
- skin
- teeth
- left
- right

Early Learning Goals

* know that print carries meaning;
* speak clearly & audibly with confidence & control;
* attempt writing for various purposes;
* use a pencil effectively & hold it effectively to form recognisable letters;
* look closely at similarities, differences, patterns & change.

Ouch!

A badge and a uniform turns your writers into doctors and nurses, recording accidents, injuries and treatments.

Resources

* clipboards
* pens
* thermometers
* badges
* stethoscopes
* charts
* x-rays (make some on OHP transparencies)
* folders and files
* mobile phones and pagers
* first aid box with plasters etc
* doctor and nurse coats

Furniture & layout

* desk and chair
* filing cabinet (in a shoe box)
* card files
* trays for papers
* board with temperature charts and medical pictures
* notice board with notes and reminders

Starting points and stimuli

1. Talk about what happens when you hurt yourself. Ask children to contribute their experiences.
2. Look at books and videos of hospitals.
3. Talk about accident forms and accidents in your setting.
4. Draw picture sequences to explain what happens when you have an accident.
5. Talk about what doctors and nurses do.
6. Use some teddies or soft toys as patients. Make records of their treatment and progress.
7. Make an accident book and record things that happen in the setting.

Extension activities:

1. Make one of the wheeled toys into an ambulance and book in patients.
2. Link the writing side of nursing in with a hospital or doctor's surgery.
3. Make medical record cards.

Vocabulary

- accident
- broken
- x-ray
- temperature
- record
- nurse
- doctor
- patient
- better
- worse
- hospital
- home
- ambulance
- bandage
- plaster
- wheelchair
- stretcher
- carry
- stethoscope

Early Learning Goals

* interact with others, negotiating plans & activities & taking turns in conversations;
* speak clearly & audibly with confidence & control;
* attempt writing for various purposes;
* use a pencil effectively & hold it effectively to form recognisable letters;
* recognise numerals 1-9.

Fire, Fire!

A fireman's hat, a phone and a notebook for addresses makes a writing opportunity with particular appeal for boys.

Resources

* fireman's hat/police helmet
* telephone, mobile phone, pager
* clip boards, notebooks, diaries, appointment book
* pens/pencils
* paper, yellow post-its
* phone book, street map
* badges
* clock, answer machine
* tape recorder with pre-recorded messages
* computer keyboard

Furniture & layout

* desk or table and chair
* screen or board with pictures, maps and words
* bell to ring for alarm
* word lists and 999 numbers
* screen or corner (with a pinboard?)
* pictures of rescue services
* key words list or labels
* list of suitable symbols and signs

Starting points and stimuli

1. Try to mak a visit to a fire station and ask if you can look at the office or get a fire officer to explain what happens.
2. Model taking an emergency call and noting the number.
3. Talk about emergencies - what they are, how you feel, what you do, who can help. Talk about all sorts of emergencies (being locked out, new babies, illness, animal rescues) as well as accidents, fires and crashes!
4. Look at a local map, mark the children's homes and setting.
5. Explain how to make entries in phone logs.
6. Discuss the importance of 999 calls. When to use a 999 call and the importance of remembering the number in case you need it.

Extension activities:

1. Work in pairs, one child each side of a screen, one phoning about an emergency while the other writes the message.
2. Tape some calls for children to listen to.
3. Link with role play, small world, puppets, outdoor play.

Vocabulary

- danger
- 999
- message
- address
- rescue
- quickly
- coming
- number
- fire
- police
- ambulance
- ladder
- help
- kitchen
- bedroom
- window
- stairs
- garage
- cat
- hospital

Early Learning Goals

* sustain attentive listening, responding to what they have heard by relevant comments, questions or actions;
* speak clearly & audibly with confidence & control;
* attempt writing for various purposes;
* use a pencil effectively & hold it effectively to form recognisable letters.

Can We Build it?

A site office, inside or in the garden, will involve children in a range of language activities including early writing.

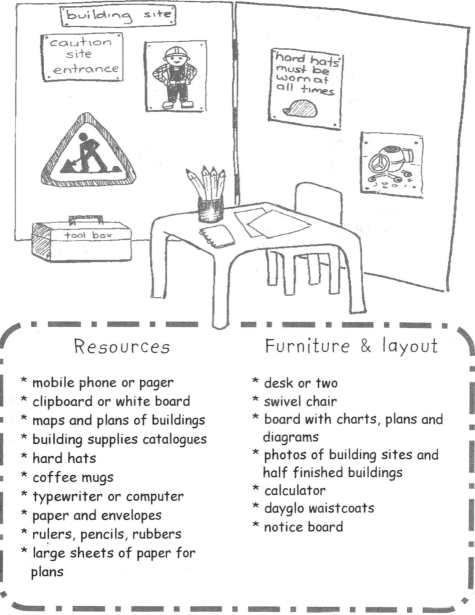

Resources

* mobile phone or pager
* clipboard or white board
* maps and plans of buildings
* building supplies catalogues
* hard hats
* coffee mugs
* typewriter or computer
* paper and envelopes
* rulers, pencils, rubbers
* large sheets of paper for plans

Furniture & layout

* desk or two
* swivel chair
* board with charts, plans and diagrams
* photos of building sites and half finished buildings
* calculator
* dayglo waistcoats
* notice board

Starting points and stimuli

1. Visit a building site if possible.
2. Talk about who orders all the things the builders need.
3. Make a list or book of all the things builders need.
4. Model some phone calls to suppliers.
5. Find some books that describe building sites and construction.
6. Draw and label some pictures of buildings, children's own houses, buildings in your locality.
7. Make lists, labels, notices, signs, instructions.

Extension activities:

1. Try making some ready mixed concrete. Use it to make stepping stones or to build walls with real bricks.
2. Link the writing area with your outside play to arrange deliveries, order new equipment, make a 'real' building site with signs, notices etc.
3. Get out all your bricks and blocks, add some small world diggers and dumpers and act out a building site.

Vocabulary

* When is it coming?
* We need.
* Send me the bill.
* hard hat
* sand
* truck
* digger
* low loader
* dumper truck
* gravel
* stones
* paving stones
* cement
* bricks
* tiles
* pipes
* floorboards

Early Learning Goals

* interact with others, negotiating plans & activities & taking turns in conversations;
* speak clearly & audibly with confidence & control;
* attempt writing for various purposes;
* use a pencil effectively & hold it effectively to form recognisable letters;
* recognise numerals 1-9.

Long, long ago

Explore how people wrote long long ago. Experiment with quill pens, scrolls and home made 'inks'.

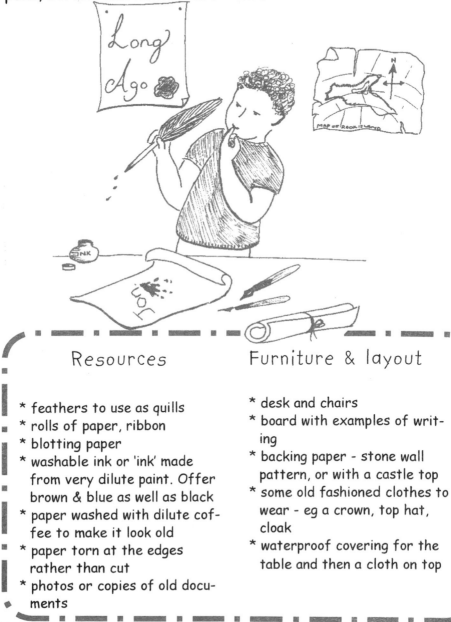

Resources

* feathers to use as quills
* rolls of paper, ribbon
* blotting paper
* washable ink or 'ink' made from very dilute paint. Offer brown & blue as well as black
* paper washed with dilute coffee to make it look old
* paper torn at the edges rather than cut
* photos or copies of old documents

Furniture & layout

* desk and chairs
* board with examples of writing
* backing paper - stone wall pattern, or with a castle top
* some old fashioned clothes to wear - eg a crown, top hat, cloak
* waterproof covering for the table and then a cloth on top

Starting points and stimuli

1. Collect some feathers (and disinfect them). Talk about how they were used to write with. Show a picture of this and model how to hold the feather. You can cut them to a nib shape if you want.
2. Encourage free play with these mark makers before introducing more challenging tasks.
3. Change the colour of paper and inks regularly.
4. Talk about blotting paper and model how to use it.
5. Talk about the language of old fashioned letters.
6. Show children how tom roll up a letter and fasten with ribbon.

Extension activities:

1. Visit a museum or library to look at old fashioned writing.
2. Make a special scroll with everyone's name on it to display in your setting.
3. Try making your own envelopes. Get some sealing wax (or use a red candle to seal them).

Vocabulary

* My Dear
* With love from
* your Majesty

* date	* king
* envelope	* queen
* stamp	* servant
* greetings	* gift
* my lord	* pleasure
* my lady	* visit
* my friend	* holiday

Early Learning Goals

* find out about, & identify some features of objects and events they observe;
* speak clearly & audibly with confidence & control;
* attempt writing for various purposes;
* use a pencil effectively & hold it effectively to form recognisable letters;
* find out about past events.

Send a message

Write some messages and send them to friends, family or imaginary characters. Or leave the message as a surprise.

Resources

* paper
* pens and pencils
* tape or ribbon to tie messages
* plastic bottles
* bags cardboard tubes, envelopes, small plastic bags
* tape, string
* photos of messages in bottles floating in water
* pictures of happy faces

Furniture & layout

* table and chairs
* pin board with examples of messages in bottles, bags, tubes, in trees, under pillows, on chairs etc

You could collect enough shoe boxes for each child to have their personal message box.

Anna	Tim	Elly	Vigo
Martin	Bruce	Sam	Harry
Mandy	Chris	Tina	Cara

Starting points and stimuli

1. Talk about sending messages, secret messages, giving people surprises, saying nice things to people.
2. Explain how messages in bottles can be used to call for help.
3. Talk about good places to hide messages so you can surprise people.
4. Try leaving a secret message for the children - a note tied to a balloon, in a bottle in the water tray outside, hung from a tree or bush.
5. Model how you can write with pictures as well as writing.
6. Suggest that children might start by writing messages to each other, putting them in empty water bottles and floating them in the water tray.

Extension activities:

1. Put everyone's names and addresses on a list in a plastic or glass bottle. Seal the bottle and float it on the beach or in a stream. Wait to see whether anyone finds it.

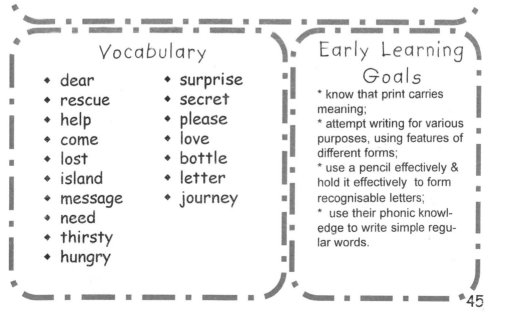

Vocabulary

- dear
- rescue
- help
- come
- lost
- island
- message
- need
- thirsty
- hungry
- surprise
- secret
- please
- love
- bottle
- letter
- journey

Early Learning Goals

* know that print carries meaning;
* attempt writing for various purposes, using features of different forms;
* use a pencil effectively & hold it effectively to form recognisable letters;
* use their phonic knowledge to write simple regular words.

Want2talk

Text messaging is a new and popular change to the way we communicate. Make a texting table for your setting.

Resources

To make the big phone you need:
* a large sheet of thick black card
* a slip in plastic wallet, trimmed to fit the size of your phone
* white stickers for phone numbers and letters
You also need paper and marker pens

What you do

Cut a phone shape from the card. Make it much bigger than a real phone. You could make several if you have room. Cut a screen and make some numbers with stickers.

Put the phones on a table and help the children to make their messages and slip them into the 'screen' pocket.

Starting points and stimuli

1. Talk about how mobile phones work, provide some mobile phones for free play.
2. Bring a phone in and ask someone to text a message to you or your group.
3. Talk about texting, and shortening words.
4. Introduce your big phones and help children to learn how they work. Give them plenty of time for free play.
5. Talk about the sorts of messages that people send - short questions, commands or requests.
6. Suggest a different sort of message to send each day.
7. Display the messages children make.

Extension activities:

1. Use the text messaging big phones in role play indoors and in the garden.
2. Offer the children some pictures to incorporate in their messages - eg a birthday cake, a person swimming, a bunch of flowers.

Vocabulary

The words you display depend on whether you feel strongly that children should only have correct and complete spellings displayed! However, text messaging is here to stay.

You could ask the children to bring text messaging words from home, from their older brothers and sisters and from their parents.

Early Learning Goals

* interact with others, negotiating plans & activities & taking turns in conversations;
*f find out about & identify the uses of technology in their everyday lives & use them in their learning
* attempt writing for various purposes;
* use a pencil effectively.

Going my way?

Making maps and following them gives lots of opportunity for writing and organising print and drawing.

Resources

* large sheets of paper
* a wide variety of pens, pencils, markers, crayons
* street maps and maps of the local area
* aerial photos
* road mats and other 'birds eye views'

Furniture & layout

* display maps, plans or a road mat on the wall to encourage children to visit the area
* make sure there is room for big sheets of paper and for two or three children to work together
* push two tables together or make this a floor based activity. Try to provide a hard, smooth surface or mark makers will tear the paper

Starting points and stimuli

1. Start by looking at some maps and talking about their features.
2. Encourage children to make maps of their journey from home to the setting.
3. Talk through the journey as they draw, Encourage them to add pictures of the features and landmarks they pass.
4. Let them talk through their journeys with other children.
5. When these maps and plans have been completed, ask them to follow a journey between two places on their map, eg from the shop to the park, the park to the library.
6. If individuals are ready for this, get them to write the instructions for routes they draw, so a stranger could follow their instructions.

Extension activities:
1. Make a huge map of the area on a huge piece of paper or in chalk on the floor or ground outside.

Vocabulary

- map
- plan
- direction
- corner
- house
- shop
- school
- library
- park
- post office
- garden
- church
- traffic lights
- crossing
- car park
- path
- grass
- field
- road

Early Learning Goals

*attempt writing for various purposes, using features of different forms such as instructions;
* speak clearly & audibly with confidence & control;
* attempt writing for various purposes;
* observe, find out & identify features in the place they live & the natural world.

So many languages

Experience of a wide range of languages and different alphabets is an important when we and all live in a multicultural society.

Writing is fun
Writing is fun
Writing is fun
Writing is fun
Writing is fun
Writing is fun

Atlas

India   Japan

Resources

* paper, card and pencils
* examples of writing in a range of different languages (each with a translation)
* newspapers, magazines, books in dual languages
* photos of people from different racial and ethnic groups
* world maps and a globe
* alphabets in different scripts
* restaurant menus

Furniture & layout

* large backing board for posters, pictures, examples of writing
* table and chairs
* dolls in different costumes
* laminated alphabets in different scripts
* costumes from different countries, particularly those represented in your community

Starting points and stimuli

1. Go for a walk to look for writing in different languages.
2. Take photos of the signs and other writing for a scrapbook.
3. Talk about different languages in your community. Invite some parents in to speak and write in different languages.
4. Borrow some dual language books from the library.
5. Try writing Arabic, Greek, Chinese or other scripts with brushes and black paint.
6. Learn how to say 'Hello' and 'Goodbye' in other languages, then find out how to write them.
7. Learn how to write some short phrases in other languages and use them in cards and on messages.

Extension activities:

1. Try a week of writing labels and instructions in French or Gujerati.
2. Find some picture dictionaries in other languages and learn how to say and write some of the words.

Some words and phrases to try.

- Good morning
- Goodbye
- Hello
- thank you
- please
- Happy Birthday
- numbers
- family names

Early Learning Goals

* naming & sounding all letters of the alphabet;
* know that print carries meaning, and in English, is read from left to right and top to bottom;
* attempt writing for various purposes;
* begin to know about their own cultures & beliefs & those of other people.

51

Secrets and spies

A fascinating mark making activity for children is secret writing. There are several ways to do it.

Resources

Method 1
* paper
* wax candles or white crayons
* very thin paint (blue/black)

Method 2
* crayons
* paper
* thick blunt pencils

Method 3
* paper, brushes
* lemon juice

What you do

<u>Method 1</u> - draw pictures, letters or patterns on the paper with candles or crayons. Paint over with thin paint to reveal the messages.

<u>Method 2</u> - cover one sheet of paper with thick crayon. Place another sheet on top and write or draw on the top sheet. Peel apart to read.

<u>Method 3</u> - paint messages with the lemon juice. Heat with hair dryer to reveal the message.

Starting points and stimuli

1. Talk about secret messages and magic writing.
2. Give plenty of opportunity to explore the methods of writing.
3. Talk about what spies do. Practise sneaking about, whispering and hiding. What do spies wear, do, say?
4. Make secret messages using the methods described.
5. Provide some spies' clothes (hats, wigs, masks, moustaches).
6. Model sending messages - by leaving secret messages for the children, asking them to meet you at a special time or in a special place. Arrive in disguise.

Extension activities:

1. Provide some carbon paper for free experimentation. Children love it!
2. Make a spy camp - in a pop up tent or other shelter, where children can make secret plans.
3. Have a secret message letter box, encourage the children to try to put letters in it without being seen.

Vocabulary

- Meet me at....
- Don't tell anyone.
- Keep a secret.
- message   • meet
- moustache   • hide
- dark glasses • behind
- wig   • mask
- cloak   • letter
- bag   • whisper
- camera   • code
- creep   • secret

Early Learning Goals

* extend their vocabulary, exploring the meanings & sounds of new words;
* speak clearly & audibly with confidence & control;
* attempt writing for various purposes;
* use language to imagine & recreate roles & experiences;
* use talk to organise, sequence & clarify thinking.

RSVP

Plan an event, then offer all the materials the children need to write invitations.

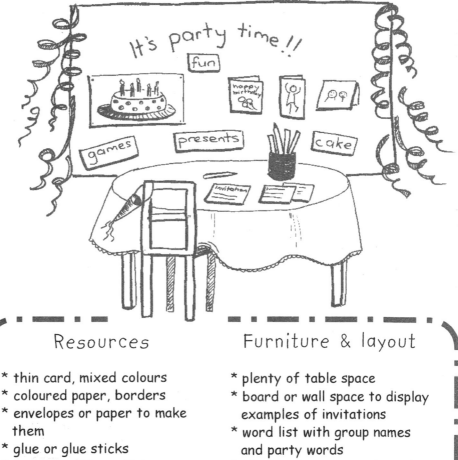

Resources

* thin card, mixed colours
* coloured paper, borders
* envelopes or paper to make them
* glue or glue sticks
* sequins, glitter, stickers
* little pictures to stick on, or fine felt pens
* pencils or pens to write inside the invitations
* list of names of the group (adults and children)
* ribbon, patterned paper

Furniture & layout

* plenty of table space
* board or wall space to display examples of invitations
* word list with group names and party words
* photos of parties and people at them
* streamers, balloons etc

Starting points and stimuli

1. Talk about celebrations and things to celebrate.
2. Choose an event to celebrate and plan what will happen. It might be a party, a concert, a birthday.
3. Make lists and brainstorms of what you will need for the celebration - food, games, seating, songs etc.
4. Collect a list of useful words.
5. Make a list of all the people who will be invited to the celebration or event.
6. Talk about invitations and how they are worded. Look at some commercially produced invitations and the signs and symbols they use - bells and horseshoes for weddings, balloons and candles for birthdays etc.

Extension activities:

1. Have a party or show for Chinese New Year, a Diwali party or other cultural festival.
2. Encourage the children to invite each other to events and parties in role play areas. Put materials in the home corner.

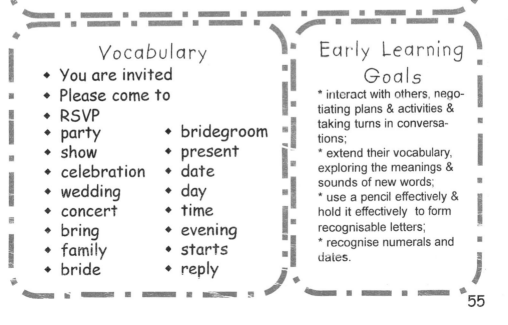

Vocabulary

- You are invited
- Please come to
- RSVP
- party
- show
- celebration
- wedding
- concert
- bring
- family
- bride
- bridegroom
- present
- date
- day
- time
- evening
- starts
- reply

Early Learning Goals

* interact with others, negotiating plans & activities & taking turns in conversations;
* extend their vocabulary, exploring the meanings & sounds of new words;
* use a pencil effectively & hold it effectively to form recognisable letters;
* recognise numerals and dates.

In character

Link your writing focus to a current book or story. Leave a few dressing up clothes ready for the writers to get into role.

Resources

A few suggestions for characters:

* teddy bear head dress for letters to Goldilocks or porridge recipes
* wizard's hats for writing spells
* Red Riding Hood cloak for writing shopping lists
* an apron for Mrs Wobble
* crowns for a royal writing desk
* giant pens and paper for a giant letter
* a jacket for Rumplestiltskin as he writes his list of names

add

* pens and other writing implements (suitably decorated)
* shaped and coloured paper
* stickers, stamps etc

Furniture & layout

* decorate the backing of the area to suit the character
* personalise chairs with fabrics, cushions, ribbons etc
* add pictures and photos on the backing board
* display lists of relevant words

Starting points and stimuli

1. When you read the story, talk about the character and how she/he might talk, walk, behave, eat.
2. Practise walking like a giant, a king, a goblin.
3. Talk about the sort of writing the character might do - lists, notices, labels, recipes etc.
4. Take suggestions for suitable writing implements for a giant, a bear, a fairy.
5 Decide what sort of chair and table they might need, the sort of paper they might use.
6. Model the posture, writing style and content of the character's writing.
7. Give time for free play in this area as well as tasks for writing.

Extension activities:

1. Make a recipe book of spells, a giant book of giant letters.
2. Use playground chalk to write huge letters on the path or wall or big sheet of paper outside.

Vocabulary

Personalise the word list with

- lists of characters
- ingredients
- food items for lists
- places from the story
- colours
- personal items linked to the story

Early Learning Goals

* use language to imagine & recreate roles & experiences;
* retell narratives in the correct sequence;
* attempt writing for various purposes;
* use a pencil effectively & hold it effectively to form recognisable letters;
* show an understanding of character.

Make a list

This simple activity is easy to set up and can be adapted for a wide range of purposes.

Resources

* strips of paper, some stapled into pads
* pens and pencils
* word lists appropriate o the focus of the list making activity
* you could make some headed lists with 'Shopping List', 'DIY List', My Favourite Things', 'Names' etc

Furniture & layout

This activity can be sited on a table, shelf, role play area, or in the garden. You may like to put some paper on small clipboards to make it easier to manage on the move.

* a pinboard with examples of lists would support less confident children

Starting points and stimuli

1. Collect some examples of lists from friends and colleagues, and share these with the children.
2. Talk about why we need to make lists and how they help you to remember things.
3. Children love collecting names, car numbers, colours, so start with some of these.
4. Once the concept of list making is established, you can change the focus by putting a notice in the area to say 'Write your Christmas List Now', 'What do we need to take on the walk to the park?' 'How many children have pets?' 'Write your name here when you have been on the computer.'

Extension activities:

1. Use list making as a group to make collections of colours, food, names, animals, vehicles. Model this on a flip chart or easel.
2. Make lists before shopping trips, outings and events.

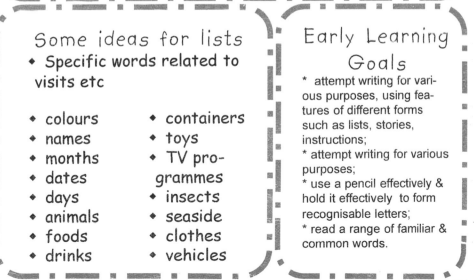

Some ideas for lists

* Specific words related to visits etc

* colours
* names
* months
* dates
* days
* animals
* foods
* drinks

* containers
* toys
* TV pro-grammes
* insects
* seaside
* clothes
* vehicles

Early Learning Goals

* attempt writing for various purposes, using features of different forms such as lists, stories, instructions;
* attempt writing for various purposes;
* use a pencil effectively & hold it effectively to form recognisable letters;
* read a range of familiar & common words.

Journey of a toy

Use an old diary to make an account of the imaginary journey of a soft toy or character doll.

Resources

* soft toy animal (Spot, a bear, TV character doll, dog etc)
* a diary or blank notebook
* special pen or pencil
* postcards, post it notes
* disposable camera
* bag or small backpack big enough for the toy, the diary and other items.

A label tied on the bag with the name and address of your setting in case he gets lost!

Furniture & layout

This writing activity will take place at home as well. In the setting, make a comfortable place on the carpet or a bean bag.

Add a backing with words, pictures and copies of relevant stories and fact books.

Starting points and stimuli

1. Introduce the character and talk about it. Give it a name and tell its story.
2. Talk with the children and get their ideas about the character. What it likes to eat, where it sleeps etc
3. Explain that the children can take turns to take the toy home and write in the diary. They can also add postcards and photos of the things they do together.
4. Make time each day to share what has happened to the toy, where it has been and what has been written in the diary.
5. During the day, the toy can accompany children's activities, which they can then record in the diary.
6. Of course, the toy will come on visits, trips and walks, and may even come on holiday with you or one of the children.

<u>Extension activities:</u>
1. Make an environment for the toy - a bed, a room or a playground.

Vocabulary

- diary
- day
- night
- stay
- visit
- bedtime
- bath
- family
- sister
- brother
- mum
- dad
- grandma
- house
- car
- plane
- party
- food
- day names
- sleep

Early Learning Goals

* use language to imagine & recreate roles & experiences;
* use their phonic knowledge to write simple regular words;
* attempt writing for various purposes;
* know that print carries meaning, and in English, is read from left to right and top to bottom.

Our new ducklings

Use a significant experience in your setting as a stimulus for writing and drawing.

Resources

This activity can follow any experience you have provided - a walk or visit, a visitor, a butterfly box, egg hatching, tadpoles, plants and seeds growing etc
* paper and pencils
* small home made books
* zig-zag books
* scrapbooks and diaries
* photos and drawings
* fact books

Furniture & layout

Try to locate the writing area near the centre of interest. Separate it by a screen where you can pin pictures, children's drawings and word lists.
* table and chairs or cushions
* pictures and word lists
* bookshelf or stand with relevant fact books
* badges with 'scientist', 'vet', 'investigator', 'reporter'.

Starting points and stimuli

1. This activity can start before you go on a visit, start the incubator or plant the seeds. Encourage the children to anticipate events by making lists and plans, and to log events as they happen - measuring plant growth, recording changes in animals, taking photos, collecting items to display.
2. Model how to write a report of a visit, by doing it together on a flip chart or easel.
3. Find fact books, posters, leaflets and other resources and discuss them as you add them to the display.
4. Share children's writing and other records in plenary times and reviews.

Extension activities:

1. Use a disposable or digital camera to make a record of what happens.
2. Make a scrapbook of pictures, leaflets, cuttings etc.
3. Keep your own diary and share it with the children.

Vocabulary

- book
- record
- growing
- day
- measure
- change
- eggs
- babies
- legs
- eyes
- swim
- jump
- seeds
- plant
- count
- hatch
- shell
- leaf
- flower
- bud

Early Learning Goals

* investigate objects & materials by using all of their senses as appropriate;
* attempt writing for various purposes;
* use a pencil effectively & hold it effectively to form recognisable letters;
* use their phonic knowledge to write simple regular words;
* recognise numerals 1-9.

When can you come?

Making appointments and writing in appointment books can be linked to many different role play situations.

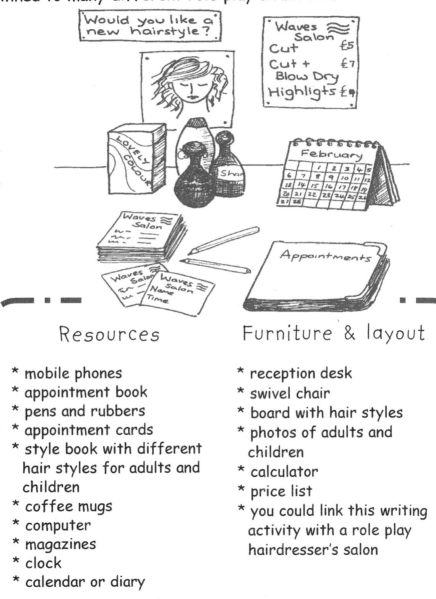

Resources

* mobile phones
* appointment book
* pens and rubbers
* appointment cards
* style book with different hair styles for adults and children
* coffee mugs
* computer
* magazines
* clock
* calendar or diary

Furniture & layout

* reception desk
* swivel chair
* board with hair styles
* photos of adults and children
* calculator
* price list
* you could link this writing activity with a role play hairdresser's salon

Starting points and stimuli

1. Visit a local hairdresser if possible.
2. Talk about what you do when you make an appointment.
3. Model what you say, and what the hairdresser says.
4. Talk about appointment books and how to use them.
5. Give plenty of time for free play before giving tasks.
6. Collect and display the specialist words for this activity.
7. Make some appointment cards and talk about reminders.
8. Make price lists and appointments for babies, children, parents.

Extension activities:

1. Make a role play hairdresser's with a waiting room and a long table for hairdressers to work on. Make sure you have plenty of mirrors.
2. Take some digital photos of the children (and their families) to make a hairstyle book.
3. Buy a couple of hairdressing magazines. Use them to make style books or laminated cards.

Vocabulary

- How can I help you?
- When can you come?
- What time?
- days of the week

• cut	• appointment
• blow dry	• curls
• perm	• special
• time	• highlights
• rollers	• full
• shampoo	• sorry

Early Learning Goals

* interact with others, negotiating plans & activities & taking turns in conversations;
* speak clearly & audibly with confidence & control;
* attempt writing for various purposes;
* use a pencil effectively & hold it effectively to form recognisable letters;
* recognise numerals 1-9;

Did you enjoy this Little Book?
Would you like to see some more?

Then join
The Little Books Club!

There's a new Little Book each month. The best way to see the new titles is to join The Little Books Club.

- *Members get each new book on approval before it goes on general sale*
- *Costs nothing to join*
- *NO MINIMUM PURCHASE*
- *Only pay for the books you choose to keep*
- *Discounts on bookshop prices, plus special offers*

Interested?

1. Tear out or copy this form.
2. Fill in your details on the other side.
3. Send it to the address given overleaf.
   (NB. no stamp needed)

Little Books Club Enrolment Form

Name (Mr/Mrs/Miss/Ms) _____

Department/Position (if applicable) _____

School/setting/organisation _____

Address _____

Post Code _____ Phone _____ E-mail _____

Please enrol me in the Little Books Club and send me all future
Little Books on 14 days approval as soon as they are published.
I have signed and dated this application, and (where applicable)
included my credit/debit card details for future payments.
I am under no obligation to accept any book, and may cancel this
instruction at any time.

Signed _____ Date _____

(Sorry - we are unable to accept an application without a signature)

Method of payment

☐ Send an invoice with each book and I will pay by cheque
(schools, nurseries & similar approved organisations only).

☐ I authorise you to charge for the cost of each book to my
Visa/Master Card/Delta/Switch card no:

| | | | | | | | | | | | | | | | | |

(Switch)

Issue no _____   Expiry date _____

📠 **fax: 0185 888 1360**   ✉ **post:**
Featherstone Education
FREEPOST MID 18874
Lutterworth LE17 4BR

**NB. This FREEPOST address is only available for Little Books Club
applications and payments.**